CABINET CARNET

ALBERT RAKOTONDRATSIMA

Archway Publishing books may be ordered
through booksellers or by contacting:

Archway Publishing
1663 Liberty Drive
Bloomington, IN 47403
www.archwaypublishing.com
844-669-3957

Because of the dynamic nature of the Internet, any web
addresses or links contained in this book may have changed
since publication and may no longer be valid. The views
expressed in this work are solely those of the author and do
not necessarily reflect the views of the publisher, and the
publisher hereby disclaims any responsibility for them.

Any people depicted in stock imagery provided by Getty Images are
models, and such images are being used for illustrative purposes only.
Certain stock imagery © Getty Images.

ISBN: 978-1-6657-3388-5 (sc)
ISBN: 978-1-6657-3389-2 (e)

Library of Congress Control Number: 2022921709

Print information available on the last page.

Archway Publishing rev. date: 12/01/2022

CONTENTS

Write acting all humans as different, having their dna code as specificity. Able to reproduce with each others, and have special needs, particular imagination, and distinct emotions.

Differences boundaries being body, nutrition, maladies. A body, flesh, lips, curvatures, ideas, belong to the similarities that human beings share.

Leeks, are eaten as vegetables, to the base of the vegetable a support leaves made called shaft forming bulrush; at the top positions greenish and tousled leaves. Vegetable is usually eaten cooked cold or hot, consume in tartes, quiches, gratins; potages, pot-au-feu, potées, salades.

A spoon of milk for the universe. A story, a movie, a song, a record, a recipe, a book, whatever, or just dust as what it was.

Experiences, fun thing about experiences; "experiences as not to be good or bad sometimes they are just experiences" as the word sounds.

The winning is not a matter of perspective, also not a told things, when a car franchise the arrival line before all other car he is winning the race. When during a negotiation, someone don't come to some the meeting, and force the adverse party to accept negotiation deal through it, he had won the negotiation. When an organization had obligated other organizations to adopt its organization system, independently of its existence, it has won the battle. The roman republic has won over other governing systems spreading the democratic to most of countries worldwide. Unfortunately, the roman empire as not survive to different threats it confronts.

The goal of this carnet, if not a treaty is to express ideas, create new ideas sometimes, reformulate sometimes, and rewrite sometimes. If not a treaty, it is a notebook on the friction of basics terms, as a field of doing and an avenue for reflection.

Write at the foot of any victory tree.

The book is dedicated to Nancy Rakotondratsima because she is my sister, but also because it is the name of a city (of France), where the people we see live.

THE METHOD

The method, there is a lot to say about the method. The method is link to the organization, to priority, to logic, and judgment. The method chapter is the first chapter of this work because it is the *foundation of reflection*[1].

The choice of the way, the manner, the path, omens of the production. In a classified model method stand as field of possibilities. The choice of the method omens the quested objective.

When a civilization favorizes achievement over smile, there is more chance that it produces an objects series than a bunch of working objects system.

For example, in a family if people always prefer the use of the bike as manner to move from two different places, it means several things.

First, the aim distance to browse has more chance to be on earth than on water. Then, it means that the calf and the quadriceps of the people in the family are more useful than

---

[1] 1637. René Descartes, <u>Discours de la méthode</u>, cogito ergo sum : doubting of everything setting the ability to think as foundation of being.

other muscles. Is there a use of a genetic bonus, or a taking advantage of a specificity.

Also, its context that they would leave wheels tracks when they are moving instead of footprints tracks.

The family could move through horseback, walk and vehicles to go from a point A to a point B. As many ways to move as there are ideas.

The method is the field of creativity expression, with performance as rating.

"All roads lead to Rome" a known sentences call back the multiplicity of wherewithal which allow to attain Rome. It is the same for an aimed goal, several methods. The difference between each method is the performance behind it, yield: time, resources, complexity. A given method could be working in a given situation or specific atmosphere and less efficient in another environment. Maybe there is a prevalent method, a prevalent method to study a topic, a prevalent method to move toward culture and logic, a prevalent method to build a human genre. A flexible procedure allowing to contact different approaches, and having as only prerogative the performance. The principal street to go to Rome.

The method is studied in philosophy to structure human mind, creating group, kind, nation. It's also studied in technique to create species groups (as well) or figure out the most performing way to achieve a goal. In strategy the method is also viewed, the case in point is differences between the multitude of learning means, pedagogy, global method, experimental method, maieutic method, and so on.

When, a method is chosen to operate about a topic, it is considered that it is the best way to achieve the goal as regards of the resources and the people who are operating.

To study an history lecture, for example, a student has several ways to memorize it. Learner can do sheets of the course and memorize the sheets. Learner can also, use reading and visual memorization, or the learner can use the auditive memorization through recording the lecture. There is different way - also "meta[2]" - to integrate the knowledge. Performance is measured through the most documented method, to each individual the best method to be used.

The main office to learn methods is university. Consequently, things that should not be forgot is that method is a learning approach to be integrated into a republic. The knowledge is a mean, as the method is a way, a "meta hodo[3]" to go in the republic.

As main office to learn paths to follow, to go in the republic, there are several things that are not said about the university. Writing a dissertation is a facts restitution, and a social exercise. Once the structure respected and learnt; the wording, the prioritizing, and the pleasure given differ. Give intellectual pleasure through contact and knowledge restitution, that are the mains dares.

The republic accepts different way to get inside the republic. The republic is composed of people, it is a state where sovereignty rest.

Method needs organization, instructions and subroutines. Within the method, interdictions and assignments.

Make a speech, make a public talk, to do an exoposé, requests method. If it could be done from the hip, often people apply a method to it. Using the method is standard.

---

[2] From the greek prefix μετά « meta- » is meaning : after, beyond, with.

[3] Formed from the prefix μετά, μέτ- meta, met- « after, which follows ». And from ὁδός, hodos, where "h" = the rough spirit on the omicron, it mean "way, path, means"

Starting with an introduction, a development and finish with conclusion.

For talking about a topic, the best way is to put oneself in people shoes first or impress them, then make the audience know more. Everyone is not keen on every bigs topics. That is why, it is important to start with an introduction and get the arguments after. It is among one of the usage of the method advantages. With the method an organization of the action.

Doing so the phenomenology alters, in it the perception, the judgement and the intentions.

The method delegates to movement, it is the keystone of every headway. Like a scander in the middle of a cornfield. The method is natural to conduct an initiative. The method is the meta. The way to follow for an enterprise, in it the starting values as fundamental stones. During the choice of a method, the landscapes viewed during the activity journey is to be thought.

The choice of a method requires reflection, observation, knowledge of the environment and especially knowledge of one own's body. Being know about one own's body; being know of the perception of it, being know about own morphology, being know about the body reflexology and its taxonomy are important points. Pick out a method for a project is a strategic gait, with unique prerogative the performance. Pick up out of a hat a method has to stay serious to be glorious. It means there is not an unique winning way to achieve an initiative. The main thing is to study and work.

The pedagogy with is the different approaches :

Negative pedagogy[4] (the pedagogy of the desire to

---

[4] 1762. Jean Jaques Rouesseau, <u>Émile ou De l'éducation</u>, defines the negative pedagogy is the education which as the tendency to perfect ourself and to elevate us.

learn), method putting the learning process in loved things stimulus.

The active pedagogy[5] (the pedagogy of the knowledge appropriation), method setting the knowledge as propriety and trust value.

The traditional pedagogy (the transmission pedagogy), method exchanging knowledge as objects.

The technology pedagogy[6] (the pedagogy by objectives, with the objective learning evaluation), the method treating the learning through stakes, creating learning cycles.

The social pedagogy[7] (the pedagogy of social being transfer only), the method protecting the social persona, treating the people in the learning process as social being.

The pedagogy of project[8] (the pedagogy through the realization of a project), the method offering the opportunity to learn through project piloting.

The pedagogy Montessori[9] (the pedagogy of full-blown

---

[5] 1782-1852 Friedrich Fröbel a German known to be a « germanic master of early childhood education » he had founded the active pedagogy.
1746-18227 Johann Heinrich Pestalozzi a Swiss who get naturalized French who had founded the active pedagogy.
[6] A pedagogy centered on student as a learner in order to effectively acquire knowledge, know-how and interpersonal skills.
1935. Pedagogy by objectives.
1958. B. F. Skinner's programmed teaching.
[7] Marxiste pedagogy consits to take in account the social personage during the teaching process.
1917. A. Makarenko
1963 Fernand Oury
1976 G. Snyders
[8] 1918. Is the project-based learning developed by William Heard Kilpatrick the article The Project Method.
The idea comes from the philosopher John Dewey, around 1900.
[9] A way of teaching created by Maria Montessori in 1907.

and by own self learning), the method allowed to learner to teach them self and find full blown through pedagogy.

The asset with the method is there is some information removed and some information added inside the process. Method is some acclimatation to some information. It helps to an individual to live in society and integrate knowledge.

A method can be beautiful, creative, bizarre. They are the qualifications for the method. Intrinsically, each human has his method, replicated, native, transposed, or thoughts.

Choosing a method is important, it helps to have some guidelines to achieve a given goal. In a fighting environment, it helps to focus on the key points, and think about the adverse, which elements would we consider to show. Method is not required at every moment, but it is great to think about it.

The method man is usually someone who is more centered on learning, more about methods than on achieving the primary goal. The method man could be me, he could be you, the method man is not uninterested about performance, nonetheless he is more concentrated on the method itself and all details which could be inside the process. Don't be the method man.

The risk of the method (etymologically way of the mind in a search work, investigation, study) raises several questions, interrogations on the human activity.

The questions on the existence of a universal and unique method, and on the diversities of the method. The scientific method is the fact example of the existence of one unique rational method. Nevertheless, the artistic activity cannot be conformed to the rigor of a method. Similar, in philosophy and concepts there is no unequivocal method to conquer the truth, if truth there is, in what does it consist precisely.

The method is a necessity to the study. The method is the result of the work, of the learning. By thoughts continuity, the method is the accession of the humanity (human mind creativity spectrum, insertion of the individual in the society, establishment of rules differentiating the human and the animal).

There is no unique method, at least if the doubt conquers the human on the way to follow, it is certainly beforehand more link to the lack of study.

When the Romans lay down the cobblestones to the antique road, they have done it to gain time and protect their merchandises during the travel. Road has been one of the most successful infrastructures of the Roman empire. It has made the empire shined and has shined as well by his performance. Romans used a specific method to fight the rain damages and the attritions caused by passageways.

The method was: dig the road, put a layer of sand, put a layer of big stones block then put a layer of small pieces of stone and the coating, the cobblestones.

The manner to build a cobblestone road as barely not changed since the antiquity.

The method defines a standard of action, frequently when a method is chosen, and when it works well, people often tend to more replicate them to solve some issues. In line with this behavior, the method is converted to some values. For this reason, it is important to make the choice of a good method, at least to acknowledge it if not adopted. Behind method, strategy and combativity.

From the time, in a battle, a general chooses some longer method instead of others faster methods at the same efficiency level, it augurs that he does not want to show the enemy his advance. In this case, the use of one method is a signal to the enemy of control of a better technology, or a better organization system, better asset.

There is a lot of psychological variables behind the method. The choice of used method, the formulation of the method, the method itself, the method devotion...

When a virgin process is discussed to the appliance of a new method process, it means there is a more marshaled way to do it. The method organizes the process and makes it standard, habitual.

Several things about the method formulation, most of the time the human mind copy the nature as model to create new models. When it doesn't come from the nature, the method gush from the imagination of the individual. There, discerning, inventive, instinct, intellectual molt, are source of the spring out new ideas.

The story of the method forgeries itself sometimes in an obviousness, making the study of the method interesting.

Method man once said, "fly logic, now watch me skyrocket, watch it[10]".

Method is evoked for all study, where there is a study there is a method. In a competition between the same competitors, the confidence and the will are often the key factor that determine the favorite contender. The process of method elaboration is a question of discernment, and understanding. Reflection and spirit come after. If there is a martial genius for the war, a genius oratory for do politics, a politics genius for governance, it seems that for the method it is the genius of discernment or the method genius.

Observation is the first step to go in the method, less

---

[10] 2009. Wu-tang, album Wu-Tang Meets The Indie Culture vol. 2: Enter the Dubstep, song U-God feat. Method.

restricted than a gaze followed by logic, it is the first require-
ment to act a method.

It is seen that the nature of the method creation process
requires a lucid mind. In such a way that being clear become
among competitive advantages. The superiority being the
only top.

There is no method without study, it is a verifiable truth.

After the choice of the method manner setting, the sub-
sequent operations are its applications, and its iterations
with them the probability to gain in speed, efficiency, and
performance. The method operation permits to standardize
action usually done innocently.

In each actions, the method follows laws and rules first,
they are principles that the exigency is to be acknowledged.
In practice, it is not always possible to rely on the senses to
adjust during an operation. Sometimes the plurality of the
reality makes the application of one method a complicated
operation. At that moment, the mind has to commit on judgment and to gamble on instinct. The method remains in one
of those extra situation objects of study as the action itself.

The exertion of the method provides advantages that
are present in various forms. Precision in method operation,
insurance in method operation, knowledge of the operation.

Do the choice of the method over relay on impulse and
senses is also to close one field in ingenuity and inspiration.
The method forgets the conditioning part of the human
journey, and leaves a large scale on the empiricisms.

The method structures the mobility of the mind first
and the mobility of the body after. By this channel the mind
avoids making suppositions inside the brain. Within the
method, the consideration is as important as the objective
and the method itself.

The destination is a part of the travel. For example, in the body management, the training habits settled, omen the type of results sought. Is this a drawing, a pulling exercise, is this a pushing exercise, is this a liveliness exercise, an endurance exercise, an explosivity exercise etc.

The body is a tool and the way it is movement foreshadows of the activity completed. Avoid pulling the ankles at the extreme of its extensions, and avoid to sit often on its front strip, are behaviors to avoid in order to get rigorous gait. In the body the articulations, the mechanic, the sense, the method.

The sense and the creativity are the machinery of the method.

The poetry of the method is to allow the possessor of the most performing method a dominance over the opponents. The significant advantage given by a performing method is the ability to out class the opponent whatever it happens, using less energy, fewer resources, less time, fewer materials. When a better method is acquired with a better technology, at that moment, it is a technology advantage, when a better method is acquired by a better comprehension, at this moment, it is a knowledge advantages, intellectual advantages.

Understand the human relation at very his thinness part are among of the cerebral advantages that can or should be got in a method operation. Terminology, phrasing, dictions, gestures, absence of gesture and silence.

When understand correctly the method offer to the operating a more complete perception of the action.

The application of the method requires discipline, organization, meticulousness. Be rigorous and rigid, by definition have a better resistance to any efforts is a benefit for method application. The method is first a defined planning to reach an objective. It is an access to an action.

The method moves itself and thinks itself within a framework.

Method applies for a specific field, to reach a defined objective, for example, to go from a point A to a point B, or execute specific actions. The method is a practical theory which deploys itself through the movement, through the vitality of the spirit.

There is no universal way to follow presently regarding the method, there is no universal method.

Nevertheless this are the things that can be said about it.

Most of the working methods if not all require movement.

A good method is structured in a logic system and produces performances.

A good method is practical.

All method is understandable.

By definition, a method is a mix of processes that are sticked together to reach a determined goal. Once set the method is decomposable and replicable.

In general, to reach goals, the method begins with model elaboration, the confrontation and verification of the model, and finishes with feasibility. When it comes about a study the common agenda is observation, hypothesis, and hypothesis verification. It is the scientific approach.

Using the method over not using it offers to the individual more confidence in motion if it is not vivacity. To be speed in a learnt method requires training, to apply a method supposes to follow orders and demands to be focused on the execution.

A good method is made to be followed by the greatest number.

The application of the method confers possession to the

one who established it. A method is the result of a reflection of a logical scheme. By definition, it is a way, a path that must be taken. In the application of intellectuals knowledge, (school, studies) the method becomes the lines of an individual to reach a given result which is retaken to him. Consequently, it is a loan, an introduction to the one who possesses it.

The power of the method is applied by its distribution or popularity and its effectiveness. The law that this assertion induces is thus this one: there is not a method strictly universal speaking, a method evolves in a field and comprises its weak points and its strong points.

The method perpetuates the logic and the reasoning. That why there is some steps when it comes to method. There is a method for almost everything, music writing, to the building of a machine, to the study of phenomenon.

The method can grant to the experimentation a moment of strong lucidity. The individual can transcend himself in the method, this happens when the will pushes him to excel, at this moment, the application reaches an optimum level of performance. The application of the method leads to the concentration of the individual's attention in the action itself to be executed rather than in the contingencies.

The method, a path, and an arrow. As a holy approach to performance: the human mind does not contain only the useful, the meaningful, the true. The approach of the method through the application of logic for performance allows to eliminate the external elements to the logic. The application of method is a path of reason and science.

The walk is analogous to the approach of the method. When walking on outdoor terrain, the body applies a particular technique to each type of ground. The mind evaluates the best way to move, either to put the whole foot or part of the foot down. Each step as an advance in the steps that constitute the method, as milestones laid down by the method towards a final destination.

The assimilation of the method to the action of walking expresses the presence of the method in our daily lives, and the meaning that is hidden behind the word. Walking is sometimes practiced without reasons; it serves first of all to move forward. Similarly, the method does not always contain meaning, it serves as an operative organization. Just as in walking the essential thing is to walk, in the method the essential thing is to do, know it.

In a march on Rome cobblestones, the footsteps of each solider resonate in the street, delivering sound and reason at the same time: impact of the espadrilles on the solid surface bring a muffled sound to the ears of citizens, and the march brings the senses of victory to their eyes. There is usually 365 days in a year. The march in Rome streets is the best way to put in perspective the method regarding the time. It asks efforts, movement, ingenuity and belong to it details. Details count.

The method is an organization of doing helping to build sustainable things. It is also an action design that give the doing action more asperity.

The Roman empire has conquest the entire Italia, a part of oriental Europe, and a part of occidental Europe. With those conquests, they have spread their values and visions. They have defined the method as a knowledge transmission manner, and goodness and truth expression and realization tool.

A method starts usually with preparation. It is an observation moment where the plan is prepared. Then in the method there is the execution. To finish with the observation again or the evaluation:

- The first part of a method is the preparation part, it is the moment of ideas and logic are to be used. To each method can be used differents logics. During this moment which is generally short, resources to be used are viewed and a strategy regarding the potential competitors can be made.
- The second part of a method is the execution, it consists to put in motion the method chosen. In this part the mind is totally focused on doing what is planned. The brain turns more in motricity than in reflection.
- The third part of a method is the examination part. The step is not always done. In a competition the part is to watch how things went for own self from the planned part to the execution and it is also about to observe what others have done compared to our process. It is the step where we are looking for improvement in the method settled.

A method exists when there is an objective set or when there is motion to do. The method doesn't exist for himself.

For complex execution tasks the method demands dexterity and ability. To fulfill those requirements the individual has to be conscious of himself, calm and aware of his environment.

Dexterity is divided into two things, ease and motricity. The ease in the method goes through mental confidence and esteem. Motricity is about keeping the muscles in shape, the articulations mobile, and his nervous system at his best level of performance. Dexterity and ability come from natural ability, and of course training.

Once the dexterity and motricity on point, the brain needs to visualize the task to run it adequately.

On an intellectual task operating, memorization is the most important part, above understanding. In the memorization process information classification and logic associations. In the method, the reason comes after the memorization, understanding follows the memorization mechanism. In addition, differents components influence to the good execution and appropriation of an intellectual method such as the fundamentals mastering.

The method is directly links with the technique. The technique provides to the method a specific knowledge based on science that help to ensure performance. The technique generally controls the method organization, when a scientific technique is picked to run a process the whole method process is devoted around it.

The application of a particular scientific method usually calls for training to be fully effective. Look at the method and the technic from a conceptual point of view determines the technic as a mean for the method. By definition, the technic exists by a scientific know how (not by itself) where the method exists by is goal and by the performance it delivers. That makes the method a purely practical and organized concepts.

The method as a strategy demonstrator. When the speed of a task reach in record delay the aimed objective, it means that the method has been better executed. Whatever it is technic advantage, scientific advantage, human advantage.

In a competitive environment a better method can be the preserve of more advance group or a more advance civilization. Do the same objective with fewer resources, less time, fewer people or with a different manner could be a signal sent to competitor of an advance we have earned.

In the method execution to reach the performance, the discipline has to be observed. If the organization is the essence of the method, the discipline is the quality to observe to have performance. The discipline applies in every step mentioned of a method, and it has to be observed in the control of the process to seek the improving points. Progress of a method come often of this dynamic, than a genius lightning. The method aims at the performance, that is why it is important to have it evaluated and to bring some improvements on it.

In this way, the method can be evoked as progress vector and as a transmission motor of good. In the method is retained what works only, what is performant. When the method is told, minds follow the logic, logos, organization outline of the method. Inside this outline, the performance and the reasoning. Follow the way of the method is to follow the scientific progress and the performance. The method is the field of the application of the scientific progress. By applying the method, is applied the logic to reach an objective with performance. The method is presented as the reason way, the science way, the truth way to the performance.

From the discipline induces the method improvement and progress to the performance.

The second quality to reach performance in the method is the observation. From the observation results the creativity. The observation is like a generator of ideas, a creativity generator. The ability to replicate, and to understand are coming from the attention paid to observe. It is one of the most important points inside the method, if the appetence to observe is not always propitious for doing, it is important for the method. After the discipline, it is the second most critical character trait to the realization of a performance in a method. Observe allows to understand better and to glimpse different manners to act to be integrated or replicated in other contexts.

Action doesn't always ask method, the action can be spontaneous, the action can be conditioned, the action can be programmed. Whatever the form of the action manifestation, it can gush out like an ardent thurible in his execution. The way an action is thought doesn't determinate his manifestation.

The method for the action, to act; more than for the ideas. It is the principle of the method, the doing for the performance. The method offers to whom master it more rapidity and control. It is the way of non-doubt due to fact of the study.

Doing is the first step in the method, the doing feeds the reflection, the doing transmits. Like an ode to the doing, the method is by definition a way among other to do. The method marshals and gives guidances, within it the logic, the organization, and a system.

The method like manner to do, a manner to think, a life philosophy. Educate with eyes, inspirate with the do, with the outlines of a method a real vision.

The method like a road to move away the human spirit form the non-reasoned. The song left by the method machineries rings like daily tune. The method is essential to classification, study a method teaches a lot about reflection path, and it is also a moment to learn and view different perspectives. From Italy antiquity, the sense followed by has produced a tremendous number of objects to work with. The antique republic has applied rules and method to conduct the empire and earn new territory. From the laying a siege to one city, to the phalanx leading, passing by education of human mind the method approach has always been a back framework. Observe, think, prepare, plan, do. The method has allowed complexes realizations, with the technic, they brought rhythm to the action. The method has inserted in culture, in philosophy, and in daily life.

Inside the rhythm of a method, the transmission of a way of think, a way to do, and a memory of traditions. Encouraging the doing, encouraging the action, the method a road to do and to accomplish.

THE TIME

The first resource of living beings, time is a duration to which one cannot cancel the meaning. A unique and absolute reference, time is irreducible and unchangeable. By itself, it is only an interval of temporality. It is articulated according to the action it witnesses. There is a time of science, an economic time, and the time of experience.

The time of science is the time of a technology, the time of a study, of a research, of a process, of a manufacture. Economic time is the time of an ideology, of a law, of a decree. The time of life is the time of an experience or the moment of a life.

It can be measured in seconds, minutes, and hours, and it can be objective or subjective. In objective time, the elapsed temporality displayed by the clock. In subjective the temporality perceived in the inner feeling of duration. Time is rhythmed by its own flow.

For humans time can be categorized into two types of duration: long time and short time. Long time corresponds to a long duration whose spread corresponds to several months, or even the temporality of one to several years.

Short time is a fast time that can be predicted and visualized on the scale of an hour to a day to three days.

In the face of time, no one escapes ripening. It transforms the living, the space and the materials. Time flows in a linear way in successive cycles.

The time flies in the action in the reflection and in resting. At every moment, it drains its flows. In the life instant, people doesn't often notice the changes that it bring with him. A furrow, a character trait, an articular change, a muscular change.

The time leaves the present moment to be grab with his heart. In the time, the past is a bygone present, the future is a present which would come, only the present moment counts.

The moment is much longer than the instant. The instant is a very short duration, even infinitesimal.

The time being the body that applies every phenomenons in the eyes of the living. Be a living in the middle of the time, to perceive it like a personal sensible reality is also a different manner to see the time: a sensibility given to each living to feel the action.

The time, the temporality, is made by interludes. Inside the time also the rhythm, the representation of self-personae, and the relation of actions between them. The time flows and doesn't own memory, it leaves sometimes some traces.

The time notion is not eternal, and it knows only how to move forward in a straight line. The time showpiece of the notion of time is change. It is the time paradox to pass linearly and continually and asks change through it.

The trajectory of a person and of an object varies with time as reference. The trajectory is the possible displacement, the most probable displacement of the object which follows his own animation. Belong to the displacement of the object the acquired strength and the emanation of the resistance of the environment.

The strengths can be a physic strength of traction, a physic strength of propulsion, a physic strength of rotation... The trajectory begins when the object is moving and it stops when the object is stopped.

Similarly, for the trajectory of a person begins at his birth moment and ends at his death. For a person, the trajectory depends to the application to movement, to work and to people met, and also bills the art and the sensible word approaches.

The trajectory of two more or less different weight objects propelled by the same strength in the same environment is more or less identical.

For a person, it is roughly the same as for the objects, in addition to be played on the will, the cleavage of porter faces, and the intelligence of the physic usage. The simplicity of a trajectory is inside the display of doing.

Expulsed with the principle of the simplicity of the ways - God as universal infinite reason[11] - and norm.

The time manipulate the personality, the norms of his person, and body movements.

The personality is the collection of physic and social character that identify a person.

The personality is a question of way of deportment - self-discipline with selfness and to other behavior - and his own physic. For males the time wilts bollocks and shapes baldness. For women time removes the ability to procreate.

The personality sends back to the image, front of the time nothing is eternal, only the time itself continues its

---

[11] 1638-1715 Nicolas Malbranche. He he lays down the principle of the simplicity of the ways and established God as origin and absolu in the word.

discharge. It is often said time is precious. When the life ends, the time continues. If the time is only perception, we can go back to the past by changing our mind's perception, our imagination, to feel again the feeling we had by decors changing, and action repetition. Unfortunately, the time is centered in the momentum, the necessity of present, the intensity of the instant, the present.

The undefined continuity of the time is like some crusher which doesn't stop to run. In a moment of a day, the time is sometimes to be savored. Savor in the doing, savor the sunshine, savor the starts light, constellations, savor the moment, savor a liquor, savor the oldness, savor self-body, savor an ice-cream, savor having sex, savor a glass of wine.

As principal resource to human, the time is the subject of reflection in wondering moments. Don't waste time, use it to do or think, or savor it. The announcement is we need you in order to do something of it, whatever work or enjoyment. The time is not stop by progress, not stop by the machines, not stop by the words, not stop by a revolution, not stop by the newspapers.

It is the writing toon of the carnet, express analysis, teaching and instruct around a fundamental subject.

The time chronos, kairos, aion in greek language is important.

The time is enjoyed usually and it is necessary to use it. Do, is essential to manage the time.

THE WOMEN

Women sources of life and natural partner of men, based on this definition for young men who are willing to conquest they are rare resources. Women condition is motley, their relation with men appears similar to "the master and slave dialectic".

In natural word there are to be dominated, raise offspring and serve the household. In modern society the women roles is more complex. Admired, desired, envied, they are unknown creature hold by the beauty. Most of the time, confused with appearance they have, the women being is a bit more elaborated.

At once charming, grace, vile, and grimy for men, the female sex has through years represented soul purity. Naivety symbol women may appear giddy, clumsy.

As a life essentials there are desired, raised delicately women are protected until they get grab by an external. Women are essentially associated with fruits, during young education vegetable and fruits are kindly apply for women.

Taste is discovered only when the first bite hit the core, some fruits are sweet and enjoyable, some are harsh as not fed meat. Ground, atmosphere make every hatches distinct.

Be raised among felines developed grace and boost glut-tony and the willing to please and to being groom.

Education, environment make a pathway, mold charac-ter sketch patterns.

Women's minds are forged with the will to be desired. Different character patterns are perceived, in modern word the will to be forth unites all most of patterns.

Historically excluded of politics in the name of his na-ture women, women are currently fighting for rights in the name of this nature; as all excluded groups.

In the society, it acts through feminism as political re-sources[12], to push specificity (also could be differences) and smooth out civilization yardsticks. Being egalitarian and dualist.

Owner of the life tool formation, the sex took is position big, second and last sex, women took the helm on lifespan. Doing so in spite of acknowledged power position.

Admitted, being a conquest field for male sex, women is sylph. Culotte[13] is the word used by the kind to describe itself. Interesting choice since the kind own a pair of breasts and an hairy bush called vagina.

"Culot" defined as aplomb audacity. Culotte[14] is also the french homonyme of panties, tight-fitting women's under-wear that cover the buttocks and the sex. Most of the time, they have a "pocket" that protects the female mucosa from bacteria and friction.

Covers for the origins of the world[15]. Intrepid definition

---

[12] 2008 <u>Sexe, genre, et sexualités,</u> Elsa Dorlin.

[13] 2016. <u>Culottées,</u> Pénélope Bagieu.

[14] Assign to the french expression "Wearing panties". It is said of a woman who is in charge in her home, often as temporal head of household.

[15] <u>The origin of the world</u>, Gustave Courbet's painting.

for a living kind who seems to have left surviving in routine. Oh, pretty woman.[16]

Flowers, thrones, brambles are female being attributes. The creature charms with her shapely, the sex beguile with her scents and ignite with her gaze.

A pair of breasts, ten toes, two arms, a pair of butt, a sexual organ, ten fingers, a back and a face are more or less the ingredients of the female sex. The type is known for her empathy, her tenderness, her sweetness, her sensitivity. Her character is next to describe this other[17] : spirit and maliciousness.

Smiling, laughing, simpering things that a woman's face is doing.

Greeks[18] had left beauty, love and strategy in women's selfness representations; and represented man with war ruse, communication and creativity. Both being the same foundation stone, gender foundations.

Woman kind is substantial, the society in a time of a generation made them stand in ample settings. From the purity of a nun, to the honesty of a coat weaver, passing to the lust of a nurse, to bravery of a judge, women are going through several circumstances.

Young boy, you will see different kinds of beauty creatures during your life spawn. Old boy, you don't have finished to find out the size of the spectrum. Young girl, your range of seat is large. Old girl, you are certainly not alone with your life spawn experience.

---

[16] 1964.Roy Orbison. Stand for his single song of Oh pretty woman released in 1964.

[17] The other sex : women.

[18] Jean-Pierre Vernant, L'Univers, les dieux, les hommes. Récits grecs des origines.

The differences between the creature and the "regular" one is the way they express themselves. Both would not express their strong desire straight way. The mores raised woman kind as daughter first and as companionship then; in the daily power game woman as politic's animal uses this condition to exercise her influence and domination. The sex is determined to use interpretations and perception to express her will.

To sum up the word with one sentence during our life spawn you would meet to kind of women: malicious woman and the good woman.

The malicious woman is defined as the woman who betrayed. A laying nature, the huge scam to avoid. The point with this type of woman is she is back-stabbing and she is duping as a friend first and then as a campaign. It is a traitor.

There is not a lot to write about the betrayer; it is like it sounds. Malignant, vicious and evil.

The second kind of women which you could meet is the good women as well-known as valid women. It is said of a woman when she is societal law respectful and words respectful. With a woman, it is the situation of a lotto winning ticket.

These are the two kinds of women you can meet. Independently of the nature[19] of the woman you met the human package remains the same: ovary, breasts, but. You may forget it, a human is first a body sharing the same feeling and the same desire.

As distinct as the spectrum of emotions in humankind, the way women handle communication is diverse.

The master word is hermeneutic as a battle for existence

---

[19] 1900.2002 Hans Georg Gadamer . Concept of dasein.

not as a to be nor an intentional presence nor narrative identity[20]. Have that mentioned, in a trading system, the political organization acts as the first truth. Politics as an essential.

Things have not to be simple, the human nature is not simple, human is not easy to pie. Nevertheless he needs to eat, to sleep, and to have his mind getting away.

The nymph is joy; sadness; and mystery. She is moving through green meadows naked and with her specific hat with her. She is watching the bees and bees are watching her. Bright in the valley. Collecting the sunshine and reflecting them with her skin. Her hairdressing as respectability and sign of her dedication. The curvature stands in nature. Within her shapeliness, her attributes and her personality. Her anatomy a moving bag of bones producing her hormones. She gets picked by a male or she is picking herself a male.

The women has to be in household the representative figure of the mother. She is nutting, giving child her breast and his first food through it. The mother is the first object of love of the child.

The "Be" and the "Bonnie", she was born from Venus, are the name given to her pair of circular chest.

It has to be known as a piece of information, women has her menstruations each periods of 28 days.

The women are usually grabbed and brings a success mark to his possessor. The trophy and the champion,

---

[20] Paul Ricoeur. He has defined the triple mimêsis theoris which enriches one's own understanding of oneself.
It is the second axis in his philosophy of citizenship, also the philosophy of action.

gathering within the victory taste. The trophy to be maintained and the champion to keep shape.

Between the women legs, place of procreation and life. Legs of the women are made of calf, quadriceps, and feet, on her feet, her toes.

THE GRATITUDE

We owe nothing to anyone, we build our lives according to our choices, our will, our abilities. I like this idea; it has built countries, forged nations and animated lives. Yet this idea is not entirely accurate.

Nowadays we like to believe that we are the sole masters of our lives, we like to think that we control everything, from our schedule to our own bodies. We have the conviction that if we give ourselves the means, the world is ours. This famous dream from across the Atlantic, rightly taken up by many people, shapes our world. We constantly want to push our limits: to walk on Mars; to secure more resources; to have more time, these are all expectations that we want to fulfill. Progress works the way we want it to work, and we try to achieve it. Sometimes the collisions get the better of us and bring us back to reality, we no longer wish to climb Everest but we congratulate ourselves on having climbed the hill we have not far from home. Sometimes we even congratulate ourselves for having thought about it, for having tried.

We do or we don't, that's not the point, because first of all we dream. This dream, this American dream, many of us believe in it. We all aspire to do better. To live better, to eat better, to do better. And very often we take the credit for this desire: we make the efforts and take the credit. After all, if another person also wants to succeed, he or she must hold on. His rise will be by the sweat of his brow, that is the principle of the American dream. Fair or not, that's how it works, yet to confine the American Dream to that would probably be a mistake. We rarely rise to the top on our talents alone. Often we seek the help of others, and most of us are grateful for that direct input to reach our goal. At that moment we show gratitude. This gratitude is customary for those who strike gold because gratitude often implies satisfaction. Thus, if the American dream has been imported across the globe, and is now available to all, gratitude seems to be the appanage of the victors. It often seems that "thank you" is reserved for the best. When we have convinced ourselves that we are going to succeed, we are seldom satisfied with trying. We fail and no one says thank you for getting their ass kicked. We reserve words of gratitude for celebrating our achievements to the point of making it a kind of ritual: we celebrate when we succeed; we say thank you after a pleasant event. Despite itself, gratitude is often seen as a response to certain events.

This distorts the notion of gratitude, which should be an attitude first. Of course, it is not about celebrating failures and defeats or losing the competitive spirit. Rather, it is about keeping in mind that being grateful is not reserved for special occasions or champions. We often forget gratitude is first of all to thank for being, for thinking, for dreaming.

THE WAR
WERRAWERRA

By definition the war is the extension of politics by other means[21], the war or werra is above all an armed conflict. In a group of organized and cultural based civilization the war is often willing to be probable, opportune.

First a duel or a fight where each taking part wants to have his own will defers and his superiority acknowledges : the war is the theater of the unlimited of the human spirit.

Next, the war, fight is subjective and randomness that the plan, the engagement, the general strategy, the attack and the defense can stake out. It is a complex exercise where the chief will and parties engagement organization and concentration make the difference. It is a old pratique and known pratique with main goal win and acknowledge the superiority.

The human life journey is regarded a certain way as a fight. A fight for resources, a fight for reproduction, a fight

---

[21] 1780 1831 Carl Philipp Gottlieb von Clausewitz, <u>De la guerre</u>.

for character, a fight for knowledge. The fight never stops, and is a necessity, doing so the war concept.

In everyday life the differences between individuals resides in the land knowledge, that is the animal of predation being, inside it the way of socializing and the ability to resonate. Socializing and resonate are the two points where it starts. By the war, the attributes start quite the same way in annex of the predation disposition, the strength physic, mental strength, and the engagement.

A matter of fact the war is not done by one individual, it is a demonstration. -demonstrating the engagement of group manifesting by the ability to elaborate tactic, demonstrating the group mass concentrate to execution, and the demonstration of the will attached to the main goal namely win and make acknowledged its superiority, they are elements that lead a group to win the war or not. - and the affirmation of self-desire, strength and political will.

From the strategy to the general engagement, to the tension and the rest, the war is advancing. Sacrifice, rationalization, artifice and ruse are also floating on the war banner.

From the head of country to the point of the bayonet, passing the trenches, cities and boundaries, the war rubs all, from the logistic, the topology, the economy, and to the treatment of all citizens.

Cold like the death, the war art knows only its own rules and strength.

The war is game of attack and defense, that the strategy rubs the complexity, and which the general genius transforms the abrasion. To be understood, the intensity and the success of a war are the arborescence of the knowledge of his chief.

Ardor, bravery, courage, are the qualities which animate his passion. It is what he carries in his engagement. His brightness in his martial spirit. All his genius, spirit and desire devoted to his task. His domination for the win.

The attack, the defense, the ruse and the rest are among the parts of the war art.

The ruse is at the foundation of the strategy for this reason we have set it at first of the position of this section. The definition of a ruse is an action intended to fool with the particularity to not miss directly to the words given. -It is what differ it from a lie.- The ruse shapes the tactic[22] and the strategy[23] after. The ruse conducts the surprise, the wariness and the clarity inside the strategy.

The attack is a full military concept, which means the advance to the enemy territory to impose our strength. It can be operated with ruptures with the enemy defense mobilization, or it can be moving in one go when there is no defense available in front of the attack.

The attack may last for a long time or just a moment : both duration being assaults time.

The defense is a passive military concept, it is the action to parry an attack. The defense concept is not without limit; it has to have ruptures otherwise there is no war. The defense concept has as aim to preserve a territory in the face of an attack. Therefore, the defense is a easier yield action tool to the conduct of a war.

The rest is the first impact of the crise created by the war. It is the result of the tension inherent to war. The rest can

---

[22] Is inside the tactic the execution of the execution of power grab and the action properly speaking.

[23] The strategy is on the engagement it self and on the adequate organisation of the army that penetrate the truth and the necessity of the war.

be between two confrontations or inside the confrontation itself.

The war is a succession of attack periods and defense periods without both their being, no war at all.

The war is atrocity and is won only with an offensive, whatever the type of offensive it is earth, marina, aircraft, nuclear, biologic... . The offensive is the unique way of bending the enemy's will and makes acknowledge our superiority.

Usually when the capital is taken the organization of a country is conquered and the war often ends at this moment. But it is not always the case, sometimes the fall of a capital doesn't mean the end of war, nor the capitulation of the battle, the war end when every enemy acknowledge the superiority and stops the battle.

The demonstration of strength has to be acknowledged as some organization kind informally and legally to avoid conflict retakes or resistance.

In a world of war, this last sentence informed about the discipline and politics logic of the fighting group. Namely, the fight motivation, motion motivations and believes, and the respect in of a political structure, plus, group cohabitation knowledge.

The victory is important, it is the validation of self-politic will above, the opponent will in terms of way of living, and it omens the ability to share a settled model by the winner.

The war for the last global episode has crystallized science progress and the human thought to what it has more to advanced.

Through his internal tension, the moment of war produces, builds, cares in order to construct a real war industry.

The war in its long practices is made of substantifications of the information and circulation of the information.

To organize the battle, they are important points. The information management, in data spited and data retained, is critical in the war conduct. Conjointly, the emotions management shown by the war leading during discussion can be a gate to get further information.

In this sense, the war has first a huge part linked to the being management. Inside everyday life communication is one of the elements that conditioning to operate the war. The way the character is managed, manifests of the general temperament and surviving awareness. Information management, its digestion, and motion through it are from the being to the character, important in competing environment. In the war, they are important element to keep eyes on, to decide and take advantage of the moment.

A war only when it concerns army with similar size and strength is uncertain.

At this moment, the general war knowledges sticking to his martial genius -courage of spirit and intellectual power - make the difference.

The chief of the army, or the general is responsible for the strategy. It role is about the use of the commitment of the armed forces to the first objective of the war. This strategy is articulated with a war plan which is a chain of operations for each war campaign. It takes into consideration the vagaries of the battlefields. To be known, the war plan is hypothetical but must take into account the ends and the means of the war when drawing it up.

The strategy is made up of the moral, physical, mathematical, geographical and logistical elements.

In its most intense unfolding, war is a series of contacts and choices, of which commitment to combat and knowledge and preparation for war are decisive elements.

Is determining at this moment, the courage, the will, the clairvoyance, the cunning and the audace of the general or the warlord. The qualities necessary for the triumph, for the climax of war are to be put in parallel with the innate nature of the leader to understand the emotions and the men.

By definition, war belongs to an element of life in society. Managing its strategy is also a very distant extension. Rationalization of the war is impressive, and what it does to physic. The war is essential to cultural centered societies, it is a distant extension. To war laws, what are authorized by the authorities.

The war collapse not only the life, it also collapses buildings, and moral strength.

As a continuity of politics, the practice of war has its rules, but the meaning of war is not. Is in war the attack, the defense, the plan of war, the destruction etc...

There is no logic behind war. To dig deeper the dialectic of the war, the war is presumably inherent to humanity and is a vector of its survival. From Alexander the great, to Napoléon Bonaparte, Winston Churchill passing by Dwight D. Eisenhower, Che Guevara and Vladimir V. Putin, Volodymyr O. Zelensky, the society as cultural oriented civilizations has never stopped conflicts.

The conflicts, and war are more than the development of animals instinct by the men, it is a part of the politic.

Of war brings arms, trenches, rifles and conquests. To make war is not a calm thing, being inscribed in a war implies a choice of rival or a choice of opponents. Because we make war to whom we look like who we consider the talents, the exhibit of achievements.

In the groove of war we are committed and we take the risk of making physical losses in the name of his conviction and his commitment to terrify the enemy.

The war can last long, or be like a lightning once engaged; it starts at the first offensive and end when the entire enemy side agrees on a defeat recognition.

ASSAY

Trying leaves the human mind in front of his weakness, his living condition. Facing up his confidence, self-willing, self-determination and self-motricity. The action to try, is to do a tentative to reach an objective, and watch what happen.

The test can be successful or unsuccessful. Success or failure, the assay is not natural decision done by the human mind.

For a group the test is easier to truck with than a individua surrounding by people.

The test is directly related to confidence and it is a hot topic to dig on. Europe the old continent has through the essay conquer the world and fill the planet with its model and its thinking design as standard.

The assay, test, try, in a human mind is often anterior to the permission or the authorization. With the good reason that the action to try is a circuitous path distant of the security. The assay character is multiple - blemish, imperfection and cross-grained, - his nature is inside the incertitude. Sometimes encourage, sometimes prohibited, the human mind moves forward with the action to try, glory or collapse.

The relief of the assay is in this double veneer. The assay, the tentative is a doubtful execution, a realization full of uncertainty.

The ability to essay in a human journey omens of his ability to move on after an inconclusive matter. Inside the assay is judged the determination and the self-confidence. The action to try is accepting the doubt, and the unpredictability of the reality of the sensible world. At this moment the action of trying become a confidence gambling and a bet against self. In point of fact, the action to essay is a self self-investment: when it works this investment can profit in success and aplomb when it fails the loss can be the failure felling and personality trait changes.

Once understand the try chain it is easier to move on with a bootless tentative. The try is a prime element to human progress. From the walk to the run to the action to fly, try is the initiative that lead the human race conquer the earth.

Hammer into a topic, hammer away something, try repeatedly something is the name of game progress by trying. The try push the human limits and make human minds pioneer. From the walk on Mars to a career choice, the action to try is the start to motion it all.

"Nothing ventured nothing gained" it's the known sentence, all gains have first shown up with a try.

There is something absurd in the action to try. To surpass self, go beyond self determined confidence cercle. To fulfill a dream, a carrier vocation, to explore a never explored zone, or just view the actual limit. Try is the anthem.

Try has no cost, confidence is not a resource nor determination, at least when things are tried and when keeping the same aim. The action to try again, and again and again is the attitude to hold to try. Hold the faith in all positions is important.

The action to try repeatedly, is not afraid of new attempts and ridicule and learn.

First to do is try and learn, the peril with the action to try repeatedly is to reiterate without learning. People learn from errors what make the tentative a failure, or learn about the operation progress. Second is improving or doing things differently the essence of trying.

The action to try is not always easy to start up, it asks self character and his own person questioning. Try is foremost for an individual outside of the regular scope of doing. Whatever how we consider the action to try is not a routine unless we are pointing the tester job. The test can be everything, it can be the moment of a material solidity measurement, and at this moment it is as well not the conventional action to operate.

Look at the light of a tester job, an object shows if he follows the manufacturing standard. The logic keeps the same, do attempts for the purpose of a goal. Score the objective remains the principal target of a test whatever try, or tentative, essay, assay, etc.

The assay can accomplish dreams when it is well executed - minutely -, the assay is often candide, innocent; when it accomplishes the dream at the first hit, it is perceived as out of ordinary, extraordinary. When it hits the goal after several tentatives, the try is celebrated. Nevertheless, the effort notion becomes subject to further discussion. When it is pointless, the try is abandoned, it's become an experience as we often do.

It is to be noticed that the assay incorporates the possibility of failure.

Contrary to the quest, which is succeed or not filled.

The assay reiterates itself with changes or adjustments to fit the settled objectives. Ordinary, at each attempts datas which could be inspected and viewed. It often said that things are not difficult in itself, the difficulty comes from the not doing tendency that humans have. A time things are initiated, the mind may confront to difficulties and it is there that datas may help by tentative adjustment or literally doing changes.

Doing first measure what have been done or not done after. The measure in the assay stands for : datas and time measurements.

In the "doing" followed by the doubt, the minutely plays an important role. It is a character trait that brings attention to slender details.

Child during their childhood are trying a lot, try forge the learning curve, and help to understand the environment and self better. It begins with the nursling who taste the milk from his mom chest and who his trying different aliments after : apple and pear as stewed fruit, boudoir when his first teeth are showing up then steak tranche when he gets older.

He also tries in sport to acknowledge others as different individuals and acknowledge his own body. He starts to run, to coordinate with a ball, with a hoop, and sometimes with strings. If he is lucky enough to be surrounded, in the adequate environment, he would even start to juggle.

It is the same for artistic field, depending of his family member and his living environment, he would try or literally learn to play music and write music. Recorder, piano, trumpet, battery, guitar, fiddle and so on, finally all instruments that could be seen in a conservatory. The male would try more some physic and fight exercise whatever frame or not, while the female would more try artistic field and acknowledge herself. Both can be inversed, it is how as a rule we are trying when we are young.

At the state of puberty the mind is trying usually his first social experimentation and go towards the other one as autonomous mind. Depending of this action of trying he would learn and adjust or not his attitude to external according to his own experience.

Lived as an experience more than a tentative, at this age, the try action can likewise affect the character and influence self in future decision made. The action of trying is included in the learning approach.[24]

At the adult age mind is not used to trying to learn anymore, whereas trying is still the action of moving from the regular tracks, it becomes then a painful way of learning. The uncertainty it induces plus the probability of do a error make it a cost full way of doing something new. It asks to be ready to be conscious of his own character and be ready to do modification on it. To an adult mind, it asks for efforts.

To a snarling soul nothing is impossible, the action to try is one of the way to make this motto true.

---

[24] It refers to the famous and well known learning by doing. John Dewey 1859 1952.

THE WORDS

The method of the logic, the method of the sense, the method of the justification, the method of the truth and elements to express emotions and ideas, words are essential elements to the language. They provide the tools to exchange and articulate itself with rules called grammar and conjugation.

In a sentence the choice of the words are important, and is even more important the respect of grammar and conjugation rules. Inside a sentence, an object, a register, and the regulation of a defined structure.

An orthographic mistake is a coarse element of a sentence. It is a bad transcription of a word. Grammar mistake is the non-respect of a grammar rule.

In the following sentence there is an example which should not to do :

> → Tell him, I am waiting for your answer.
> Dis lui, j'attends ta réponse. Dic illi, expecto responsum tuum.

In this sentence we have not an orthographic mistake but a grammar mistake. By misuse of language, there is a him, lui, instead of me, moi.

The confusion of the pronouns him and me has leads to a grammar miss. The polyvalence of the language to express itself allows the sentence to be understandable and to understand its object. The sentence intention is nevertheless different, in fact the language plurality leaves to imagine different intentions when the non-regulated usage of grammar structure.

POLYSEMY

The polysemy is the propriety of a word to have differents meanings, the polysemy of a word differs with the usage of the language.

A word which has different meaning can lose some signification with the time if it is only used in a manner. Also the polysemy of a word can add more significations to it dependently of his usage in the actuality.

LANGUAGE CHARACTER

A language is a set of signs used for communication. It is a social activity. It differs from one country to another and it is generally organized in 3 modal times.

The language tells about the culture of a country and the character of its inhabitants. The place of the verb in a sentence indicates for example the importance of doing in the culture. The use of negation relates to the detail of the dialectic. The way the language is spoken tells about the attention of its inhabitants to the care of the truth.

In the Chinese language, for example, one can affirm a fact and its opposite in two consecutive sentences. The attachment to truth is not linear as in European languages.

LANGUAGE DIFFERENCES

A language differs from another language by its grammar and by the letters that compose it. A language can be simple, rigid, rigorous, organized, complex, flexible, continuous to oneself or discontinuous.

The tons of words, from one language to another are different, they make the authenticity of the language and its particularity, to each sonority a particular pronunciation. From a language to another a more organized structure to express the same sentence, that qualifies the language.

Example :

English:
I am the one who does it.
Français:
C'est moi qui fait.
Latine :
Praesent quis convallis mi.

AN UNIVERSAL INTERFACE TO GET THE MAXIMUM OF EMOTIONS

A language is made to be talked, to each language some sound and specific structure that identify it. Sound expresses one character and a nature.

Like an animal expressing his nature with the sound it emits, a language, a culture expresses his nature throughout the structure chosen and sound expressed. To go more deeper in the universality, the word sound transmits an emotion, and the word itself. With the translation the universality of a word is totally reached.

The word through its existence allow to understand every living and emotions transactions.

This way through the word's interface the emotion structure, the face structure, and the culture structure.

CONSONANTS DOUBLING

Omened instead of ommened is a commonly done spelling mistake in the spelling of a word. It is the consonant doubling. To date, there is no defined rule in the English language to avoid this type of mistake.

THE FORGOT OF THE -S IN THE THIRD PERSON OF THE PRESENT

In the present the third person takes a -s, not putting it at the end of the verb is a fault. It is a grammar fault and is a huge mistake.

THE RESPECT

As essential element in everyday life the respect is an important topic. More learn by experience than in theory there are however tricky points about respect.

The respect is taken not given : it is a common sentence that is more than often than not expressed to relate about respect. It means that the respect is an obligation.

Coming out of the latin respectus signifies regard and consideration, the respect is the abstraction of action nor offensive judgment toward the valor of a person or the valor of an object.

Everyday, we act with respect when we say "hello" to someone, when we finish a dish as a guest, when we punch a boxer, or when we say thank you. We acknowledge the valor and don't offense it.

The respect is to act abiding by the moral right. Act with respect is to act by the love of the humanity and according to this duty not by this duty.

The respect is a part that is structuring one organization and is a portion of discipline. The respect doesn't make organization nor lead to discipline but it contributes. Respect helps in hierarchy and safeness.

In modern society, the respect is first of all consideration about others and paying attention about others, recognition self in others. Therefore, acting with respect is a difficult exercise to be made - demand to avoid act by the respect and compute his self-esteem -.

The respect starts with the moral and with the acceptance of others valors. Whatever it is strength respect, degree respect, age respect, rank respect, muscles respect as long there is an element which has to be considered there is a potential respected value.

The respect is not submission, it is a responsive acceptance. It necessitates the sensibility and the intellect of the individual.

Ordinary, the respect is expressed without a second thought it is almost a social reflex that declares the institution's respect.

During the middle age the concept was assimilated to "courtly love" and "authority fear".

The courtly love is the attitude hold by a men nearby a women, founded on honesty and courtesy in order to reach joy and happiness.

The authority fear is the act to submit in front of thought a superior perception. The superiority can be though divine - by born privileged, or by spiritual believes -, it can be the superiority of a better capitalism power or the superiority of better strength arguments.

THE FOOD

Vegetables, fruits, meats, groundnuts, salads, tubercles are natural aliments eaten by the human mind. Sometimes cooked or sometimes fresh, they are eaten by the human as food for being strength sources and nutritional needs. The food bring power and vitality, once ingest in the mouth it is transformed by the stomach to become nutrients, blood nourishments.

The role of the food is very important for humans, and for living in general, it is the fuel which keeps the organism fine and running. Some of them has particular property and benefit that help the body to strive on externals offenses or dysfunctions.

Aliments can be steamed, boiled, cooked, or grilled to be eaten. Within each cooking method there are advantages and inconveniences. The texture, the taste, the nutriments ratio and the flavor vary depending of the way of cooking.

The human usually eats three times during the day, at the beginning of the day, in the middle of the day and at night beginning.

To each aliments, an optimum way of cooking to bring

out the best flavor of the food. With way of cooking a the flavor, a taste and a specific vitamins compassed in the food.

The regime of a person defines his body structure and influences his character and his kind.

Aliments are medicine, natural treatment to the body, and design the metabolism. Through alimentation, a human survey his weight, his health and also his humor.

One of most famous recipe is spaghetti, it is a recipe of dry pasta which originated in the twelfth century. Coming from a mix of wheat farina and eggs drained, pasta are a very popular aliment in Europe and all over the glob. It is the spaghetti bases. It is eaten the morning, at noontime, and at evening, is sometimes added to it condiments to embellish the taste. Like the flattery to eloquence, condiments are not the main dish in a meal; nor a necessity, they are mingled to aliments to enhance the taste. In a spaghetti recipe, condiments can be thyme, pepper, and salt, they are necessary to a good spaghetti dish.

A well-known spaghetti recipe is the recipe of bolognese spaghetti, a dish usually eaten at noontime area and served hot, eaten alone or in group, it is a mix of pasta, beef meat and tomatoes. The recipe is highly calorific. The beef meat is known to be strong in proteins which is good for muscles and keep body hot. The wheat pasta are high in proteins, carbohydrates and lipids, which play an important role for muscles as well.

It is said sometimes that we eat forms, it is told because the forms count in the in the appetite and emotions while eating.

In the eaten process, the human mind identifies the color and forms he is seeing, then associate in plus of the envy to eat some mood in it : desire, joy, proudness, sadness, sworn, laconic, competitiveness.

At this moment the eating process serve to conditionate self toward a particular emotion, to be more seek by the body. The food helps to shape the body design, and emotions are doing the same. While eating the mind can condition itself to emotions loved and emotions not loved in order to motion in the modern society.

Eating is essential to the human mind and also are the emotions, muscles tonus and emotions holding are the two elements giving energy and strength, they are complementary.

The case in point of this point is there are words that encourage us, and words which are not, that can push self to crying and paralyze. Some words are emotions molding, and are stimulating the organism to his excellence, other not.

The food, helps the body to sustain to it self, and participate to his performance. It regulates the effluvium of the body and bring the drive to life.

Like a pharmakon, at the same time positive and negative, food is poison and remedy at the same time to the body. To each individual his specific need and organism.

The body transforms a lot of things to gas or energy, the spectrum of what can be eaten is very large.

To be highlighted is, there is barely positive aliments and some almost only positive being aliments.

Eating a pizza: a pizza can be bitten hot or cold, it also can be eaten the morning or at the midnight. It constitutes one of the most famous dish ever made, for love of the food people can put whatever they want inside. A good pizza encompasses mozzarella, cheese, tomato sauce, olive, and good ham.

Eating is a need and a pleasure, it is a true way to get pleasure.

Aliments are prepared to form meals, a meal usually consists of a starter, a main course and a dessert.

The tomato, both a vegetable and a fruit, is eaten as a starter, main course and rarely as a dessert. The food contains umami, one of the five basic flavors. It can be eaten as a slices, squares, triangles, coulis, juice or just as a whole. Tomatoes activate the taste receptors in a modified form mGluR4 and mGluR1, as well as the type 1 receptors (T1R1 + T1R3) to get the umami taste.

The tomato is good for lips, for the skin tone and brain through the nutriment it provides and sensor it stimulates.

The leek, consumed as a vegetable is known to brighten up the voice and stimulating brain by heating it in the frontal zone when eaten raw or half-cooked. The vegetable is beneficial for the intestine and helps to retain urine, embellishes the face by removing redness, pimples and soothing insect bites.

The eggplant and the bell pepper, they are two vegetable witch are inserted in starter or in main courses, if not eaten as main component of a recipe. Those insertion have to be noted, in the human diet, it is normal to have sometimes mix of aliment for a recipe. Eggplants are rich in potassiums, coppers, manganeses and seleniums, and help to evacuate toxins accumulated by the body. It helps the liver and the biliary vesicle. The bell peppers, are rich in vitamin C and his good to fight against bad cholesterol and help the organism with the anti oxidants that it contains.

The list of vegetable could be eaten is long, to each vegetables his advantages and disadvantages. To compass the human journey with vegetables met and rendez-vous of emotions are important point to take in account young male and young female.

The food as necessity and maximization of the life experience. Eating bring energy and also feeling, experience it.

MATH

Mathematic is a discipline invented in by first man in Africa, and have perpetuated from this age. The math is a discipline that is met in most of studied field, and is shared in several parts : arithmetic, algebra, analyses, geometry, math logic, probability,...

- The geometrie is the discipline of space study, it can be worked in one dimension, in two dimension, in three dimension or more dimensions.

    The current number of workable dimensions is to unlimited number.

    Geometry is the reference discipline to work in any space. Is space the extend limited or unlimited where a distance can be traveled. Geometrie is equally the major discipline to work with forms and appearances. It is not the unique field that encircles the work on material and distances.

    From, line passing by the triangle, to the square, the trapeze, the rectangle, the pentagon, the hexagon, the hexagonal, octagon, enagon, decagon, undecagon, tetragon ; the geometrie is the area of execution of form, and production of designs. Genesis, of architectural work and aerodynamic production, the geometrie is the field which works what is seen, inside is directory : symmetry, a line, segments, points, perimeter, aerea, volume...

A geometric line is a not limited line, a geometric segment is a limited line, acknowledge it. As well, during your work or anywhere else, you could be asked a geometric half-line, it is a half-closed line.

With the geometry there is also the trigonometry field, field engages in the angle of triangle study and go with the concept of sinus, arcsinus, cosinus arccosinus, tangent arctangent, it is inside the geometry vocabulary.

- Algebra is the study of the operations of the math as number, as operating property and as mathematic systems. Algebra is the first tool to compute reality, and to modulate a system. It is the best field of mathematic to transpose and solve problem from the reality. "It has to be divided 100 brot of bread between 10 mens containing, a sailor, a fore man, an guard, all of three receiving a double piece. What should it gives to each?" one of the most famous algebra problem, it is an archive from the british museum of london found in -1650 BC. Algebra goes from polynoms study to equation study and is by definition is present in almost all math domains.

- Analyses is the field of the math which define the notion of limit. The limit is the moment when a function doesn't reach a determined threshold, it is set in a settled abscise point like a line which can not be passed it can correspond to the maximum or the minimum of a function depending of the function nature. The notion of limit can be hanged with functions, sequence, series...

- Arithmetic is the field of the math which applies on the study of the on entire numbers and quantity. It about the study of behavior of sequences of number, larges numbers, and series of numbers, the discipline is very helpful in cryptography and calls more than often to basic operation rules addition, soustraction, division, multiplication to operate.

- Probability is the field of mathematics which study the possibility of any event. Usually, it is computed from the ratio of probable cases to all possible cases of an event.

- Math logic is the field that study the math like a language that applied to think, it the study of frequent connectors that are : the disjunction (or), the conjunction (and), the negation (inverse), the implication (consequence), the equivalence (equality), the exclusive (separation).

- Math holds also other branches like the pure mathematics and the applied mathematics, that work on of mathematics motion by other motivations that practical application and the association of math to models applied to others fields like physic and informations, network, informatic, finance...

The math is like a language a poetry, that resonates with the reality of the world and reasons inside things. It calls to reason what is what makes us human. First to know about math it follows its flows and follows the song of logic. It accept imagination with intelligence and inventiveness, and can rely to instinct to resolve. Math is at beginning about solving than map out a logic, in math solutions matter the most than the way to get there.

Therefore, math can be made from the hip without errors with the right culture. Math helps a lot to build the civilization, through its applications, it builds bridges, buildings, roads and trains.

Through centuries, more than thousand of mathematician have work on the discipline, producing theorem and axiom. Math is field which seek sens behind reality and for itself. The discipline work with rational and logic.

Rational is argumentation following a given sense, what is rational do not stand for itself and is frame in a fence of a moot point.

Is logic what stand by itself in nature, like the nature of though, the logic is material tool to express oneself. There is several types of logic, the absurd, the contraposite, the equivalence, the recurrence, the reprocity, ….

When follow-up in an argumentation with truth, the logic become a demonstration. In math demonstration are used to indicate the validity of a reasoning, a theorem.

Sole, subject englobing many fields, form the solar system study, to mineral like schultenite study, passing by the social interaction and portal archway construction, mathematic is recognized.

Math and the logic its brings with it, helps to express ideas the best way they can be express. With numbers, math brings, system understanding, datas, measurement, quantification and precision to field it is applied on. To the speech, it brings logic connector and diverse way to argument.

Mathematics start with axioms and principles they are

undemonstrable sentence that everyone acknowledge as truth.

The history tell that math have been used before writing, first count have been made in Africa using bones.

The math comes from the greek μάθημα máthēma which mean "knowledge, and science" it has came from the verb manthánô which mean "learn", and is written mathematique with the symbol μαθήματα. The greek root has give birth to the adjectif μαθηματικός mathematikos, which have meant "related to knowledge", then transform to "in relation with the mathematical science". In latin the adjectif have been transliterated into mathematikos, which have been translated in the word mathematic as we know today.

The pyramid of Cheops in Memphis.

The cheops pyramid or the giza pyramid is the graves of the pharaon kheops and length 230 meters. The pyramid have been built at -2560 BC and hold tons of mathematic reference: for example, the gold number is found in the tilt ratio of the pyramid, and pi is found in the half perimeter of the base minus the height length.

The Alexandria Lighthouse.

The pharos of Alexandira was build during of the reign of Ptolemy II Philadelphus between -280- 247 BC. During the -300 BC the pharos was the tallest made structure of in word, his structure base was a square, his first colone was octagonal colone, and his point is a peak. Symbol of human technical advancement, the building of the lighthouse have used mathematic to stand on its foundation, and served alexandrie town and government of its out reached.

The tomb of Mausoleus at Halicarnassus.

The tomb was built between -353 BC and -350 BC, the building measured 45m of height. The construction has been admired for the sculptures and his finesse. The building had 36 pillars and was in his conception a beauty of proportion, relating the presence of mathematics inside it.

The Temple of Artemis in Ephesus.

It is simply a geometric form construction, a rectangle built in marble dimensioned of 137,74 m of length and 71,74 m of width. The temple is known for it size and for the beauty of the building, from a simple geometric form it has been made one of seven wonders of the ancient world.

The chryselephantine statue of Zeus at Olympia.

The statue of Zeus is one of the seven wonders of the ancient word which contain a very few element of math inside, what is can be mention is the pedestal, the statue height was 12,4m, and it has been a very famous statue during the anticity. The statut have been built in -436 BC and was knew to hold the victory symbol in the right hand.

The Hanging Gardens of Babylon.

The garden of Babylon is one of the seven wonder of the ancient world, its has been built in earthwork style, and it can be referred to the arithmetic sequence in mathematic. The earthwork have called to the strengths comprehension and for that was passing by strength study using the operational mathematic operations.

The Colossus of Rhodes.

The Colossus of Rhodes is a statue of helios the lord of sun, his height is 33m and it has been build on the year -292 BC. The legs of the of the statut is triangle shaped, and on the peak in the head there are peaks remind mathematics.

Through ages mathematics have accompanied building and doing. It has to be observed that there is no nobel price of mathematic, the field has not being selected to this honor, instead mathematician are gratified by the medal fields or the abel price.

In fact, math can be found everywhere from the babies tooth growth, to they own growth, passing by his first word told and his first girll firend, math can modelize almost everything. The discipline is the foundation of many and is a main branch of knowledge.

THE INSTITUTIONS

An institution is an organization which is anchored in mores. It can be a politic party, a group of though, a group of profession, or it can be told about one practice, a club, a company.

It is often said that an institution is immutable, it is the foundation of a society. Institutions crystallize in the form of rules for the use of given social practices.

There is no republic without institution nor society without institutions. They concentrate the foundation of culture and reproduce the systems that move it. They have normative and regulatory functions. The republic is an institutions lot, institutions codify the republic, inside the institutions greatness the republic greatness, its standards, also institutions limits.

An institution is first a group of individual sharing the same interests and codes. An institution often defends an ideal and rights, and has the particularity to renew their membership each year or each year's cycles. An institution as every organization lives for itself.

Belong to institutions symbols and customs, they are means and ends of an institution.

Symbols can be a motif draw, hands signs, clothings, rings, tattoos, or also just a specific paper or card. They are the visual attributes that signify the ownership to the group.

Customs are rituals that are used by the organization to proclaim an event or observe a habit. Custom are ceremonial usually use for folklore, and disseminate a part of the organization inside the members: transmitted in it values, community, ideal image, network usage, and face character. Ceremonial are used to hit this exchanges objectives and acclimate to the group.

An institution often covers a huge amount of people moving in the same sense and having the same commitments and convictions.

The institution is organized with an administrative part, an operational part and a membership part. The administrative part is which decisions are made and government of the institution discussed. The operational part is the part where the institution uses means to answer its commitments and convictions. The membership part is the most crowed part and regroup all people who are engaged to convictions and have signed to the institution.

The more people are going through the institution, the more people should adhere to its commitments and convictions. To continue of this, the expansion of his power and his practice.

As portions of the society and the republic, institutions exercise their power in its vision of the world and its construction. Institution sets systems and ideals, in their will the motion of their power.

Institution is the opposite of intuition conceivably. Is

an institution what is instituted, established, ruled and is an intuition what is natural, instinctive, spontaneous. They sound the same way, in the orthography are seen the same with the -sti difference.

In fact, they are not that different word, an intuition can be instituted and institution can be intuited. First by habit and second by analogy, both are solving an issue ideas.

Chameleon does move in their environment by camouflaging their entire body. They hide their natural green color to borrow the environment color. They are in the top 10 of camouflaging animal, and get it perceives as such.

To be an institution, it has to be recognized as an institution first.

The institution follows fluids laws rules, once the code known and embraced everything is running in one sense to express the potential of the institution. To the individual, the institution split the human representation in two different characters. The persona and the personae, his main work is to shape the persona.

That why the chameleon example is relevant to point out an institution limits. Once codes learnt, the institution become more a show tool than a commitment and ideal tool. Also rather than become a member of the institution at this moment, it is better to borrow the code and use the camouflage to motion.

Articulated in the modern world the organization in institution is a model of exercise of the power as well as the royalty. The model allows an ideal to spread and to undertake human realizations, the institution exercises the power by the structuring.

Institution are source of money, power and is the tool to serve the republic interest. They motion the society with the boundaries they set and to the ideal they commit or not. The institutions exist for their duty, and pledge.

In an institution there is a lot of things done, and in their commitment also.

In the city, the republic, the institution grouping aims at educating the sensitive and intellectual intuition. In the facts it leads the actions towards ideals and commitments.

An institution is often a place first, for this reason an institution is « meeting » . This is one of the main advantages of an institution: a place to get to know other people with the same aspirations as oneself. The institution as a place has also the advantages of allowing the exhibition of knowledge and beauty within it, and offers the symbolism of a sanctuary in its representation.

The institution is defined by the living, it recognized to itself, it recognized through transmissions done by the senses of communication. The importance of an institution is recognized to :

> the time it has existed.
> the number of brilliant people attracted to it
> the amount of money generated
> the size of it community

An institution is governed by an administrative group in which there is a president, a director and possibly a board of directors.

The president is the one who is at the head of the institution, he literally serves as the headliner of the institution. By interpreting the ideals of the institution, he prints his dough and chooses the direction in which he wishes the institution to move. The president is voted or appointed, it is a temporary position, the title of which can be life. He is the one who gives impetus to the institution and to the center of its choices, through him everything is done.

The director is the head of operations, he chooses the concrete positioning of the institution and directs the direction of the institution.

The Board of Directors regulates, monitors and directs the institution, it is organized in a collegial manner.

According to the president, the institution takes on a rhythm, and sports a tempo.

In institutional establishments, actions with a normative and regulatory function are carried out and exercised. Through its functions, the institution establishes a convention of standards.

An institution is by definition political: it exercises power in its organization, and it obtains behavior from people in contact with it that they would not have adopted spontaneously.

The power of an institution is measured by the number of significant people actively included and engaged in the institution. As well as the money generated by the institution itself.

Because of the importance of the organization of an institution, of the number of individuals that it composes, it is difficult to undo an institution.

An institution is the fulfillment of human culture, they are engaged in ideals and transform the world according to their ideas. The founding of an institution is, as all organizations, to perpetuate itself and print his footprint to the world by his activity.

The object of an institution can be sportive, social, politic, medical, educative...

The institutions live by their memberships more than their ideas, of this fact, they subsist for and by the money that they generate.

The ideals are directionals motions of the institution, the individual convene around them, the ideals are engraved in the republic draw. The life of institutions subsist first by their members.

For an institution, the input of links of all of their members is important, it distinguishes it from a simple association of persons. Links created by symbols and rituals are structuring for the institution.

First element of the link, the symbol from the greek sumbolon is historically, an object cut into two pieces for recognition. It is a conscious element or figuration referring to an unconscious content.

Second element of the link, rituals or mores from the greek ethos express a piece of the moral of the institution. In the practice of the ritual and mores, the institution makes live a part of itself.

To be noted, the reflection field of an institution is narrowed to a specific field. The reflection field is to define it is specialized. From the limited topic worked by the institution, is sprayed the mass of necessities to enhance his project : it is observed a stronger complexity.

The knowledges of the institution are wherefore propped to answer its necessities with more precisions.

The institutions in technology area computes his power by the innovations done and by the number of inventions set, the number of talented people attracted and money generated are as well important to the institution but don't count as evaluating metrics.

Globally, to act his power, the institutions use its

standards, its network, and the importance of its notoriety - membership and popularity -.

The standards often work out as model which its diffusion indicates the inscription of the institution in the game of authority in the thinking moment. The more an institution is instituting standards or a norm fast, the more it prestige increases, within it his leadership.

Its network deploys itself through the recognition of persons who are members and their mutual assistance, mutual frequentation, and mutual gathering. Its network gives contacts and allows one person to be included in a community which counts. It is a good tool to exercise power, when an institution have in its own many people in position power it allows it to print its mark and its will memorably : achievement of unique things, achievement of unique record, achievement of unique story, appointment of people from its midst to singular positions.

The notoriety is the amount of people aware about the institution. It goes from the membership number to the number of people who had heard about the institution brand. When the institution has a good public image the notoriety is a very good tool to unlock closed doors and a very effective business card to bring with. To power, the notoriety helps to have the consent, the acquiesce and the permission. The notoriety helps in the adhesion of a project or procedure : it omens good work angle.

To choose an institution, its ethic, its moral count as the basic values which are carried by its. To be aligned with them and acknowledge them are relevant points, if work is obligatory. Little boy, little girl, institution label doesn't mean work label. Like a white folder to go to work, it helps to get inside the office but is not needed to do the job. If most of the time it opens door, to have any called institution background is not a guarantee. It is not a guarantee for employment, not a guarantee for competences, nor a guarantee of network. For good or for bad it is a fact.

That is what an institution is.

Institutions do, achieve projects and shape the individual persona. Great achievements have been done by institutions. As an aggregate of structure composing the republic, be inside an institution is the to make the bet of corporation in first to enter in the republic. It is one way to go in it.

There institution for all most every field, there is institution in education providing scholarship, there are institutions in administration providing legal knowledge, there are institutions in military providing career, there are institutions in politic providing ideologic group, there are institutions in business providing experiences, there are institutions in medicine providing work, there are institutions in every field. In the institutions there is food and drink, primordial is to do, to each field diverse forms of these institutions.

The institution as mesh of republic structures and as a way among enter in the republic and do inside it.

DER CHAPTER
MEDICINE

The most, interesting, exciting, and promising topic, medicine is the area which has any things to dig, and any things to grind, in the next coming years. With the culture deconstruction, the science advancement, the number of people rising, medicine is the topic to study.

New materials allowed to operate the human kind entirely to all his body pieces. From the vaccine production to the advancement in heart operation, passing by skin and knees operations. Medicine is promoting for the human race, as kind and as human nature changes. At the writing moment the known medicine allowed to break the dna sequence to treat a disease. Within, human nature remains the same, politics and social animal.

If culture has shaped human civilization, it has also shaped human body and human well-being. Inside the culture habits, inside the culture grimaces, and emotions management, inside the culture: body, gazes, and discussions.

Is the medicine the final solution for the human being, the final chapter to study?

Is the human kind destined to live one hundred years? Is the human race could live without illness with is antibody only? Is the human would liberate through medicine? They are medicine main dares. Is medicine der chapter?

Being able to shape his own corps, to leave him as it is it - going through disease without incommodities-, to heal is body without leave his liberty, that are the medicine offers to the human kind as perspective. The human brain promises in term of medicine area a multitude of scaling progress.

Medicine as source of human progress and as light to follow.

Many things are covered by medicine, biology, spirituality, astrology, chemistry and mathematics. The topic is promising and in constant evolution, its looks like to the principal branch of the tree knowledge, surrounded by others branches, to make it fully understood; and you, medicine? Are you the last topic to understand: der chapter?

Nutrition is the thing to be evoked first when medicine has to be thought. Leaks, eggplants, and tomatoes are vegetables and fruits whom could be eaten by divers manner. Grilled, sauté, or bake with water, they can be ingested in different recipes. Braised and eaten, the question is knowing aliment properties, and eat the adequate aliment. Nutrition is the study of the assimilation of aliments inside the organism. That why it is important to be interesting in the cooking mode and legumes and fruits characteristics. Cooking and alimentation habits, they are the main lever to think about the nutrition in everyday life. The nutrition is especially used by people to maximize their bodybuilding, their lifestyle and their own organism pathogens treatment. Learning to use the best diet is a serious medical defy.

Nested in habits the emotions cycle management, having as function: spirituality's and beliefs's care.

Marshal emotion is the first key for well-being. It's also a walk to take in charge own self-medicine. The body talks, it is sending small messages to express information, if you didn't know about it, be pleased to hear about it now. Through meditation, yoga, and gymnastics you maintain a good body shape, and listen your body to move it to its maximum potential. Through mind and body care, master your mind and emotions. Emotions are sources of many body changes from posture to skin, to brain reflection, to body behavior and body taxonomy. This way, it is paramount to call upon own body understanding and emotions understanding. Understand own self-emotions, own-organism, self-body, self-taxonomy is a main challenge.

The brains are connected to each other. In each other the mind reflected itself and extend, in this sense sharing good emotions became a wellbeing topic. With the amount of living humans nowadays, around 7,87 billions, it is important to think deeper about culture and emotion management. Like homeopathic pellets and antibody principles, there is something to think - if it's not to do - behind the number of raising humans around the globe as a system opportunity; one main challenge.

From Greek, medicine was founded on the search of an ideal saint, since then the discipline has entered in roman civilization and spread worldwide. The Greek have done a lot, wherever medicine topic or derivative topics from it - pharmacy, maieutic, kinesiologist dentist, nursing, surgery... -. The main Greek craftsperson in medicine was Hippocrate from Cos, he has developed Greek scientific medicine through a cluster corpus of a set of treaty, from the V century BC to the Hellenistic period he has been the origin of the building what is called now a medical school library. The library belongs to several authors and several books versions are in it. It is the library the *Corpus Hippocraticum*[25].

Since Hippocrate and Greeks, the discipline has incorporated several improvements in terms of measure and organization, of ethics and reasoning.

The medicine is not the negation of the life, or it is, it depends on the view perspective. Work, study, ingrate diseases to live longer. To date, the discipline is major challenge for the human race.

Medicine like the topic of life. The medicine which heals and leave the human race on the top of species hill. It is the topic which study the human body in is dynamic. Molecules, granulates, capsules are swallowed from particles culled. Syringes, needles, thermometers are tools inserted in the human body to operate body evaluations or to inject medicaments.

Looking at the animal world, from reptile world to mammal world, living has created some surviving system the human can replicate. The human race has through millennium changed his body for an intellectual dominance over his environment and sometimes have operated medicine operations to go through those changes.

Medicine, medicine, medicine, are you the last topic to study, are you der chapter?

Surrounded of many topics, culture, philosophy,

---

[25] The Hippocratic Corpus, the <u>Hippocratic Collection</u> or the <u>Hippocratic Canon</u> is a collection of about sixty books on medicine written in the 3rd century.

chemistry, mathematic, spirituality, is it the medicine the higher branch of the knowledge tree, which will give the human nature a liberation fruit, a new savor to life, the time of a life cycle to make the human, the sapien sapien different.

The human as accomplished conqueror, threatened by nothing immobile with the sole prerogative of time.

If it has been made some small and big marbles, the nature as also made difference between each human in term of personality, organism, character and body. Those differences extend to the nation level, and until the cultural level. To each groups, differents adaptations levels to the nature and the world. Is there better marble for human to play, there is, back on the color of the marble, back on the size of the marble, back on the material of the marble, there is better marble to play with than others. Same logic for humans, some are made ideal size to fight the nature, ideal skin, ideal eyes, ideal hair, ideal nose, ideal fingers, ideal legs, ideal knees, ideal toes, ...

There is better human than other to adapt to the nature, there is also better human than other to enter in the republic. The challenge of the medicine is maybe to advance those ideal further and push others towards the ideal goal. It can be made through looking around the branches surrounding medicine, it is a method to avoid complexed mind and, also permit to operate quickly.

There is a lot to discover in the human mind if not to re-explain, in term of spirituality, helping the mind to operate in name of the good. Medicine, solutions for mind, pills to balance human nature.

Understand the beauty of human body nature and understand the human mind nature to heal it better are main challenge for the medicine topic.

The body flux and taxonomy have to be rethink and reexplain, with the impact of emotion on own-body on everyday life they are huge topic that are not well known for now. The oriental medicine has concepted a lot on body flux, particularly the Chinese medicine. The Chinese medicine has founded a system of the organization of the human fluid flux. Inside fluid, chakra and energy, the qi. Presently, the Chinese medicine is practice and heal stress diseases as other diseases. For taxonomy, the model used today is the model inherited form the history, European model outcome from German totalitarian vestige. The model is based on the body usage possibilities and measurements. Besides, it associates to the face a huge importance in the human being, inside its rigorism. In the face trait the character expression and the to be.

Those two fields of body understanding are also challenges to light up and understand better.

Finally, it remains to make a remark, the medicine discipline around of the human body as principal subject, building the culture, the language, the way of living, the study, the food, and the reasoning, having as unique law, the law of the body may act as last human chapter. As a branch of the tree knowledge, it is one of the most promising topics, if it is not the last to study, der chapter. When the knowledge of the body and the knowledge of the mind is conquered, it fades away with its questioning and discomfort about selfness. Conquering the medicine topic alongside the emotions comprehension, the body comprehension, and the mind comprehension would leave the feeling of completed task.

«We sell where we come from»

Printed in the United States
by Baker & Taylor Publisher Services